BANANA BONKERS!

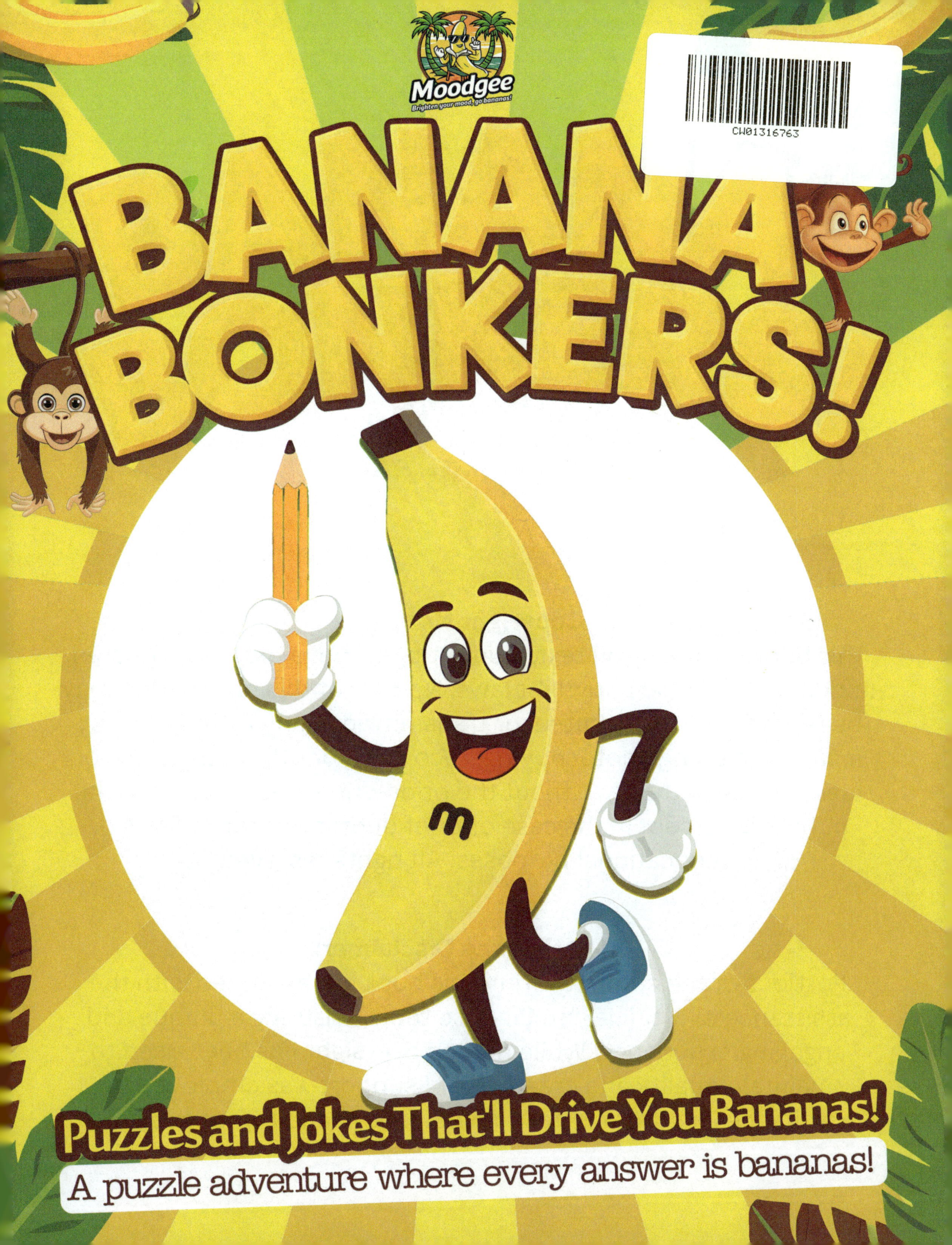

Puzzles and Jokes That'll Drive You Bananas!

A puzzle adventure where every answer is bananas!

Copyright Notice:

This book, including all text, illustrations, and layout, is protected under international copyright laws. No part of this publication may be reproduced, distributed, or transmitted in any form or by any means, including photocopying, recording, or other electronic or mechanical methods, without the prior written permission of the publisher, except in the case of brief quotations for reviews or educational purposes. All rights reserved

AI Assistance Disclaimer:

Portions of the content within this book were created with the assistance of artificial intelligence tools, ensuring a unique and engaging experience. While human oversight has been used to maintain quality and creativity, AI support was employed to enhance illustrations, text development, and layout design.

Property of the Chief Banana.

_____

_____

_____

Moodgee
Brighten your mood, go bananas!

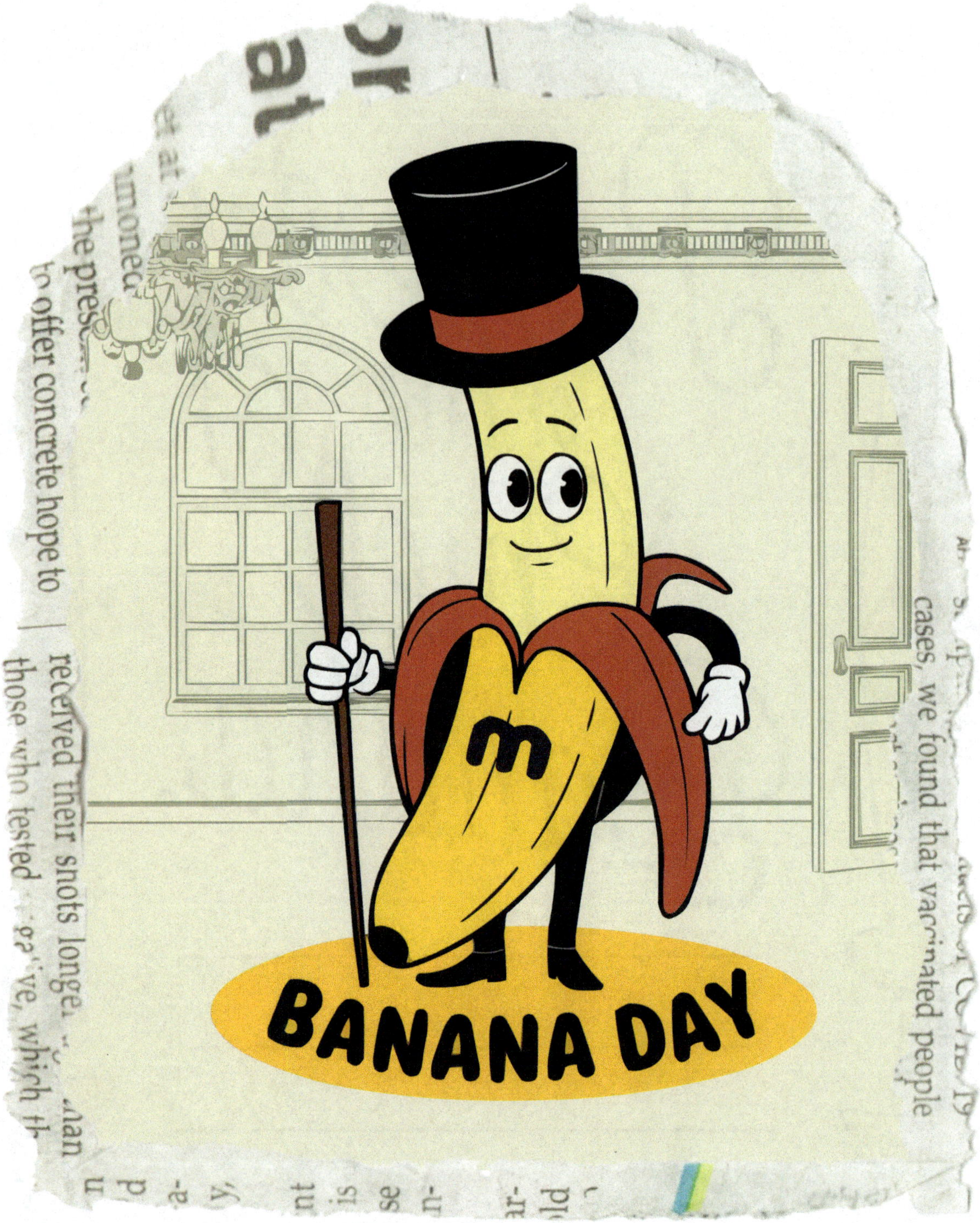
BANANA DAY

Welcome

Welcome to The Big Book of Bananas: A Puzzle Adventure!
Hello there, fellow puzzle lover! Welcome to the wacky, wonderful world of bananas! In this book, you'll embark on a wild adventure where every puzzle, riddle, and challenge has one simple, delicious solution—BANANA!

Whether you're a fan of crosswords, word searches, riddles, or Sudoku-style games, you're in for a treat. But beware—things might get slippery, so keep your wits about you as you peel back the layers of each puzzle. And don't worry if you slip up—after all, what's an adventure without a few banana peels along the way?

So grab your pen, sharpen your mind, and get ready to go totally bananas! By the time you finish, you'll be a certified Banana Master, and who knows? You might even learn a thing or two about everyone's favorite yellow fruit along the way.
Now, are you ready to jump into the wildest, most a-peel-ing puzzle book you've ever seen? Let's get started!

Solutions pages and sudoku icons (stickers) at the end of the book

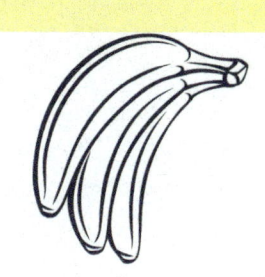

Banana Laughs

Banana Laughs

1- **Why did the banana fail its driving test?**
   - *Because it couldn't find the right peel!*

2- **Why did the banana go to the doctor?**
   - *Because it wasn't peeling very well!*

3- **What do you call two bananas?**
   - *A pair of slippers!*

4- **Why don't bananas ever get lonely?**
   - *Because they hang out in bunches!*

5- **What's a banana's favorite gym exercise?**
   - *The banana split!*

6- **Why did the banana go out with the prune?**
   - *Because it couldn't find a date!*

7- **What do bananas say when they pick up the phone?**
   - *Yellow?*

8- **How do bananas prefer to travel?**
   - *In a yellow submarine!*

Banana Laughs

1- **Why are bananas never late?**
   - *They always split on time!*

2- **What's a banana's favorite music?**
   - *Anything with a lot of appeal!*

3- **What did the banana say to the monkey?**
   - *Nothing, bananas can't talk!*

4- **How do you make a banana split?**
   - *Tell it a really funny joke!*

5- **What's a banana's favorite dessert?**
   - *A sundae with extra appeal!*

6- **What kind of key opens a banana?**
   - *A mon-key!*

7- **What's a banana's least favorite fruit?**
   - *Lemon—too much competition for sour looks!*

8- **How do bananas make decisions?**
   - *They weigh all the peels!*

Banana Quiz, Riddles...

Banana Facts or Fiction?
CAN YOU SPOT WHAT'S REAL OR JUST BANANAS?

1. Rubbing a banana peel on your teeth can help whiten them.

   FACT   FICTION

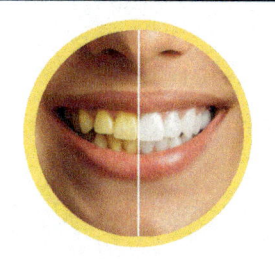

2. Bananas are naturally purple before they ripen to yellow.

   FACT   FICTION

3. Bananas are technically considered a type of herb.

   FACT   FICTION

4. Bananas can sing to each other in low frequencies that humans can't hear.

   FACT   FICTION

5. Eating too many bananas can actually make you feel sleepy.

   FACT   FICTION

11

Banana Facts or Fiction?
CAN YOU SPOT WHAT'S REAL OR JUST BANANAS?

6. Bananas are native to Antarctica, where they thrive in the cold.

FACT   FICTION

7. The word "banana" comes from the Swahili word for "slipper."

FACT   FICTION

8. Bananas are a great source of vitamin B6.

FACT   FICTION

9. Bananas are the fastest-growing fruit in the world, growing up to 3 inches per day.

FACT   FICTION

10. Bananas have been used as a form of currency in some cultures.

FACT   FICTION

Banana Riddles:
CAN YOU GUESS THE A-PEEL-ING ANSWER?

It's a fruit that's soft and sweet.
It can be mashed, sliced, or blended.
It has a peel that you throw away.
It's known to be a comedy prop in old skits.

Answer
_____

It has no legs.
It's shaped like a crescent moon.
It's a common snack for athletes.
It starts out green but ripens into yellow.

Answer
_____

It's a fruit that you peel.
It's great in bread, muffins, or a smoothie.
It's curved and easy to hold.
It can be green, yellow, or even brown.

Answer
_____

It is yellow and curved.
It grows in bunches.
It is often found in smoothies.
It's a favorite snack for monkeys.

Answer
_____

It is yellow on the outside.
It's white on the inside.
It is often part of a split with ice cream.
It's curved, and you can find it in bunches.

Answer
_____

Banana Riddles:
CAN YOU GUESS THE A-PEEL-ING ANSWER?

It is eaten as a snack or added to bread. It's often mashed for baby food. It's high in vitamin B6. It comes in bunches called 'hands'.	**Answer** _____

It's a go-to snack after workouts. It helps with muscle cramps. It's yellow and sweet. It's a fruit that monkeys are known to love.	**Answer** _____

It is yellow with a soft inside. It's popular in tropical climates. It's used in cartoons to make characters slip. It's curved and sweet.	**Answer** _____

It can be dried and eaten as chips. It's naturally sweet and soft. It's yellow and curved. It's known for being a staple fruit worldwide.	**Answer** _____

It can be found in different colors, like red or blue. It's a common fruit in tropical regions. It's known for its thick, yellow peel. It's sweet and soft inside.	**Answer** _____

Banana Quiz: Choose Your Banana!

Welcome to the ultimate banana quiz! Every question has one simple answer—banana! But can you spot the right one? (Hint: it's always banana!) Go ahead and show off your a-peel-ing knowledge!

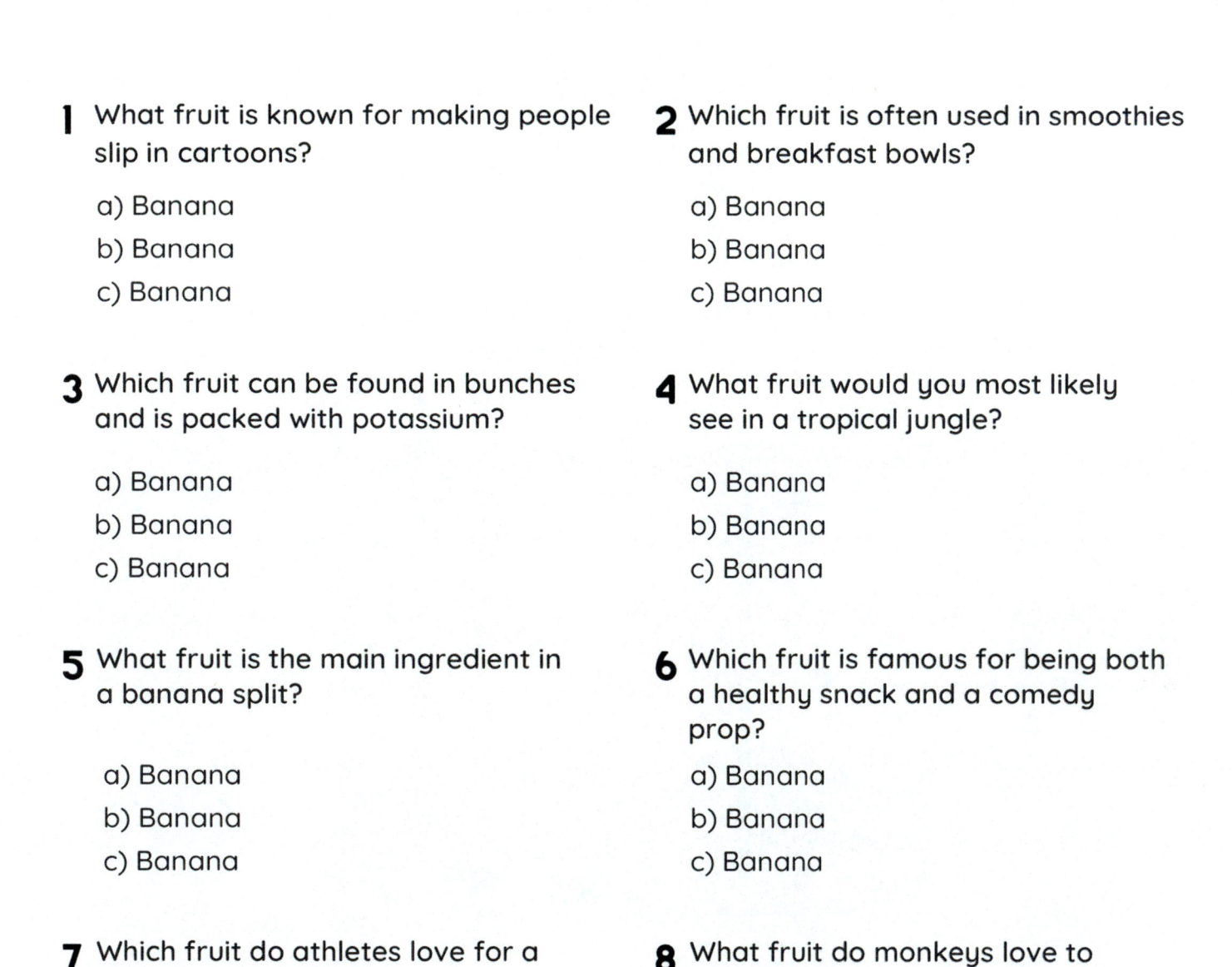

1 What fruit is known for making people slip in cartoons?

a) Banana
b) Banana
c) Banana

2 Which fruit is often used in smoothies and breakfast bowls?

a) Banana
b) Banana
c) Banana

3 Which fruit can be found in bunches and is packed with potassium?

a) Banana
b) Banana
c) Banana

4 What fruit would you most likely see in a tropical jungle?

a) Banana
b) Banana
c) Banana

5 What fruit is the main ingredient in a banana split?

a) Banana
b) Banana
c) Banana

6 Which fruit is famous for being both a healthy snack and a comedy prop?

a) Banana
b) Banana
c) Banana

7 Which fruit do athletes love for a quick energy boost?

a) Banana
b) Banana
c) Banana

8 What fruit do monkeys love to munch on?

a) Banana
b) Banana
c) Banana

Banana Puzzles

16

Go Bananas! CROSSWORD #1

Across

4. A yellow fruit that's curved.

5. A fruit often found in smoothies.

6. A fruit that monkeys love.

Down

1. The main ingredient in banana bread.

2. A fruit that's both a comedy prop and a breakfast ingredient.

3. Something you might slip on in a cartoon.

Go Bananas! CROSSWORD #2

Across

4. A fruit used in a popular dessert, often paired with ice cream.

5. A fruit that's high in potassium.

6. A fruit that goes great in a split.

Down

1. A fruit that can be found in bunches.

2. A food that's both a breakfast staple and a comedy prop.

3. A yellow fruit that curves.

Go Bananas! CROSSWORD # 3

Across

3. A common smoothie ingredient.

5. A food often associated with humor and clumsiness.

6. A yellow fruit with a distinctive shape.

Down

1. A fruit that monkeys love.

2. A fruit used in bread and muffins.

4. Something you might slip on in a cartoon.

Go Bananas! CROSSWORD # 9

Across

3. A fruit with a peel that slips.

4. A fruit that's high in potassium.

5. A food often used in baking.

Down

1. A yellow fruit eaten by athletes.

2. A fruit that's curved and often found in bunches.

3. A fruit known for being a comedy prop.

20

B-A-N-A-N-A Hunt: Find Your Favorite Fruit!

PUZZLE #1

Ready to go bananas? This word search is packed with everyone's favorite fruit—BANANA—hidden not once, not twice, but EIGHT times! Your mission is to find all the 'BANANAS' hiding in the grid, so keep your eyes peeled (pun intended!)

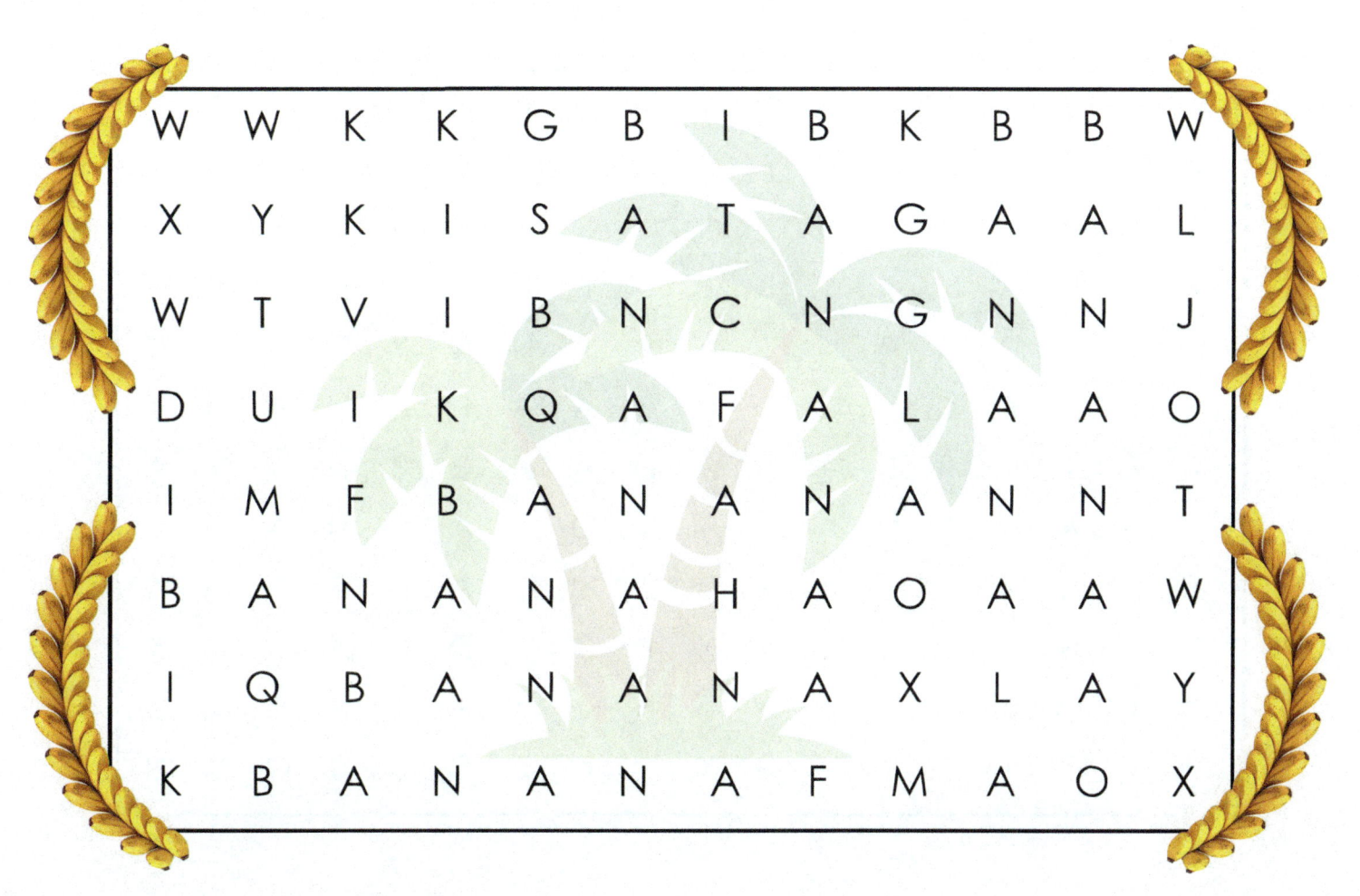

```
W W K K G B I B K B B W
X Y K I S A T A G A A L
W T V I B N C N G N N J
D U I K Q A F A L A A O
I M F B A N A N A N N T
B A N A N A H A O A A W
I Q B A N A N A X L A Y
K B A N A N A F M A O X
```

Find the following words in the puzzle.

Words are hidden → and ↓

| BANANA | BANANA | BANANA | BANANA |
| BANANA | BANANA | BANANA | BANANA |

21

B-A-N-A-N-A Hunt: Find Your Favorite Fruit!

PUZZLE #2

Ready to go bananas? This word search is packed with everyone's favorite fruit—BANANA—hidden not once, not twice, but NiNE times! Your mission is to find all the 'BANANAS' hiding in the grid, so keep your eyes peeled (pun intended!)

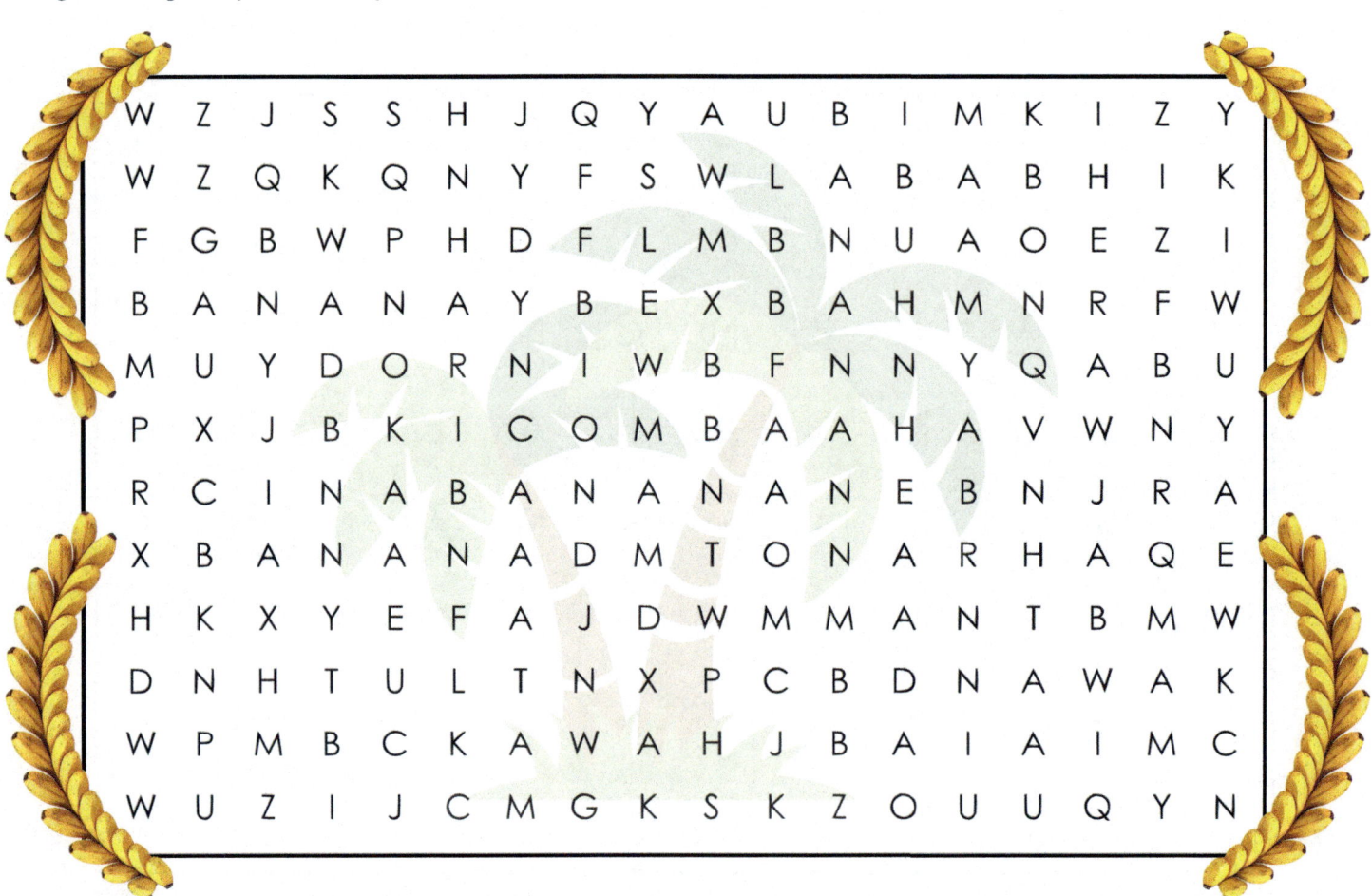

```
W Z J S S H J Q Y A U B I M K I Z Y
W Z Q K Q N Y F S W L A B A B H I K
F G B W P H D F L M B N U A O E Z I
B A N A N A Y B E X B A H M N R F W
M U Y D O R N I W B F N N Y Q A B U
P X J B K I C O M B A A H A V W N Y
R C I N A B A N A N A N E B N J R A
X B A N A N A D M T O N A R H A Q E
H K X Y E F A J D W M M A N T B M W
D N H T U L T N X P C B D N A W A K
W P M B C K A W A H J B A I A I M C
W U Z I J C M G K S K Z O U U Q Y N
```

Find the following words in the puzzle.

Words are hidden → ↓ and ↘

BANANA   BANANA   BANANA   BANANA   BANANA
BANANA   BANANA   BANANA   BANANA

22

B-A-N-A-N-A Hunt: Find Your Favorite Fruit!

PUZZLE #3

Ready to go bananas? This word search is packed with everyone's favorite fruit—BANANA—hidden not once, not twice, but 17 times! Your mission is to find all the 'BANANAS' hiding in the grid, so keep your eyes peeled (pun intended!)

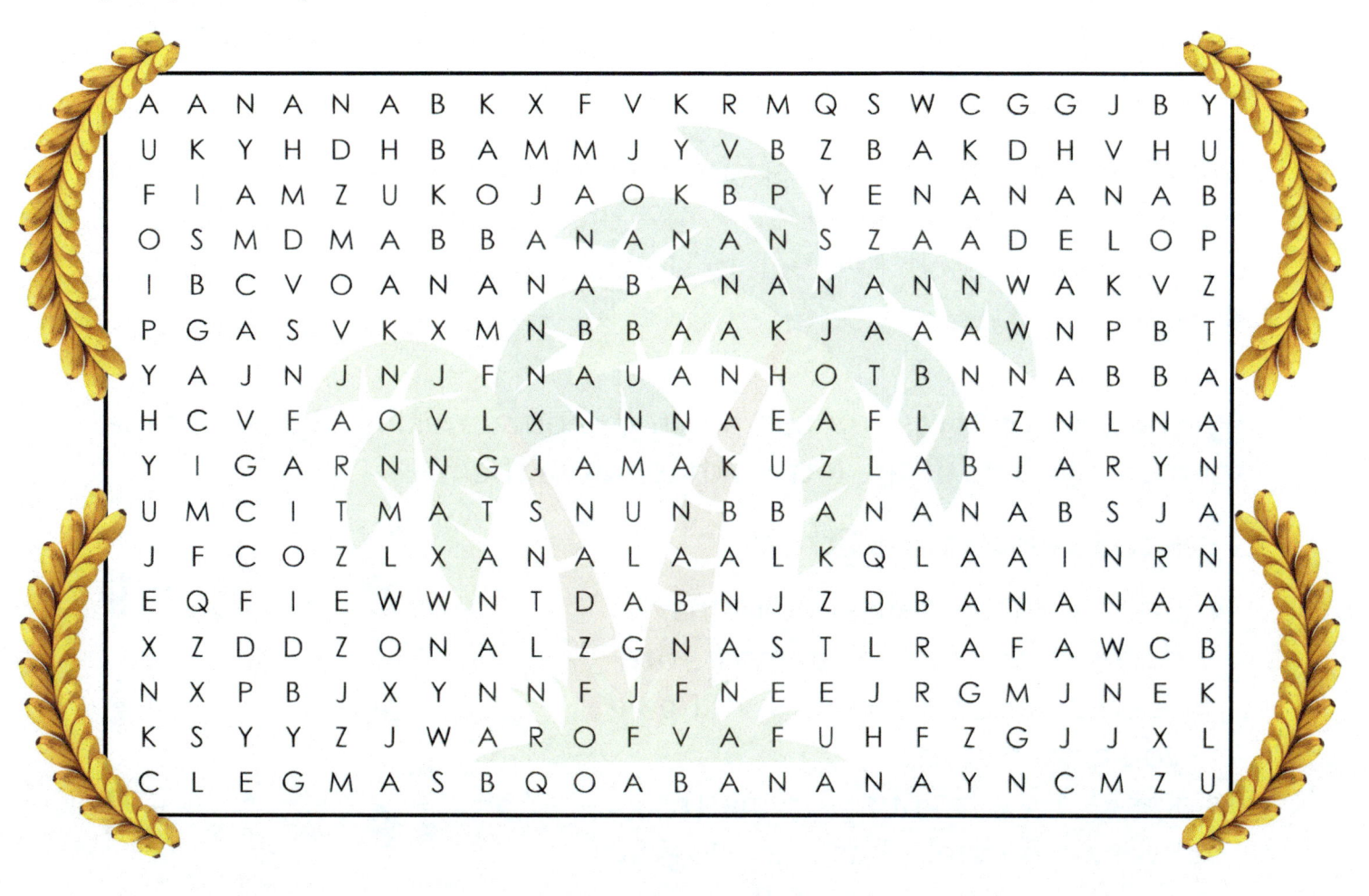

```
A A N A N A B K X F V K R M Q S W C G G J B Y
U K Y H D H B A M M J Y V B Z B A K D H V H U
F I A M Z U K O J A O K B P Y E N A N A N A B
O S M D M A B B A N A N A N S Z A A D E L O P
I B C V O A N A N A B A N A N A N N W A K V Z
P G A S V K X M N B B A A K J A A A W N P B T
Y A J N J N J F N A U A N H O T B N N A B B A
H C V F A O V L X N N A E A F L A Z N L N A
Y I G A R N N G J A M A K U Z L A B J A R Y N
U M C I T M A T S N U N B B A N A N A B S J A
J F C O Z L X A N A L A A L K Q L A A I N R N
E Q F I E W W N T D A B N J Z D B A N A N A A
X Z D D Z O N A L Z G N A S T L R A F A W C B
N X P B J X Y N N F J F N E E J R G M J N E K
K S Y Y Z J W A R O F V A F U H F Z G J J X L
C L E G M A S B Q O A B A N A N A Y N C M Z U
```

Find the following words in the puzzle.

Words are hidden → ↓ and ↘

BANANA BANANA BANANA BANANA BANANA BANANA BANANA
BANANA BANANA BANANA BANANA BANANA BANANA BANANA
BANANA

Banana Sudoku:
A-PEEL-ING PUZZLES WITH A TROPICAL TWIST!

How to Solve Banana Bonkers Sudoku!

Welcome to the world of Banana Bonkers Sudoku! Here, we've given the classic number puzzle a fruity twist. Instead of numbers, you'll be working with our special banana-themed symbols or letters. But don't worry—it's as easy as peeling a banana!

The Goal: Fill every empty space in the grid so that each row, each column, and each smaller box (4x4 or 6x6 depending on the grid size) contains each symbol or letter exactly once. No repeats allowed!

Symbols or Letters: You can solve the puzzle using either banana-themed symbols or the letters that match them.

Tips to Go Bananas Over:

- Start with the rows, columns, or boxes that have the most pre-filled symbols or letters. It'll give you a head start!
- Keep an eye out for patterns. Every puzzle has a logical solution, so think carefully before placing a symbol.
- Don't get frustrated—peel back your worries and try again if you slip up!

🍌 = B   ☀️ = U

🐵 = M   🍌(peel) = L

🌴 = P   🍌🍌 = C

🥤 = S   🌴🌴 = H

          🌺 = F

Ready to flex your puzzle-solving muscles and have some fruity fun? Let's get cracking and go bananas!

SUDOKU 4X4 PUZZLE #1

			P 🌴
P 🌴			S 🥤
	M 🐵	P 🌴	

Use the provided symbol key (at the end of the book) to cut out and place the icons, or simply use the letters that match each symbol to solve the puzzle. Just remember: each symbol or letter must appear only once in every row, column, and box. Are you ready to bring order to the banana jungle? Let's go bananas!

SUDOKU
4X4   PUZZLE # 2

Use the provided symbol key (at the end of the book) to cut out and place the icons, or simply use the letters that match each symbol to solve the puzzle. Just remember: each symbol or letter must appear only once in every row, column, and box. Are you ready to bring order to the banana jungle? Let's go bananas!

SUDOKU
6X6 PUZZLE #1

Use the provided symbol key to cut out and place the icons provided, or simply use the letters that match each symbol to solve the puzzle. Just remember: each symbol or letter must appear only once in every row, column, and box. Are you ready to bring order to the banana jungle? Let's go bananas!

SUDOKU
6X6   PUZZLE # 2

Use the provided symbol key to cut out and place the icons from next page, or simply use the letters that match each symbol to solve the puzzle. Just remember: each symbol or letter must appear only once in every row, column, and box. Are you ready to bring order to the banana jungle? Let's go bananas!

28

SUDOKU
9X9 PUZZLE #1

F					M		C	
C					H		L	U
	H			B			F	M
	U	H		F				
M							H	
		B		M	C	S		
			M		B			
		U				C		F
	L	C	U					H

29

SUDOKU
9X9 PUZZLE # 2

					F		C	
	C			U	B			
						S		B
								L
P			H					U
	M			S			P	
	B	M						
F					C			M
	U				P		L	

30

Color & Be Inspired!

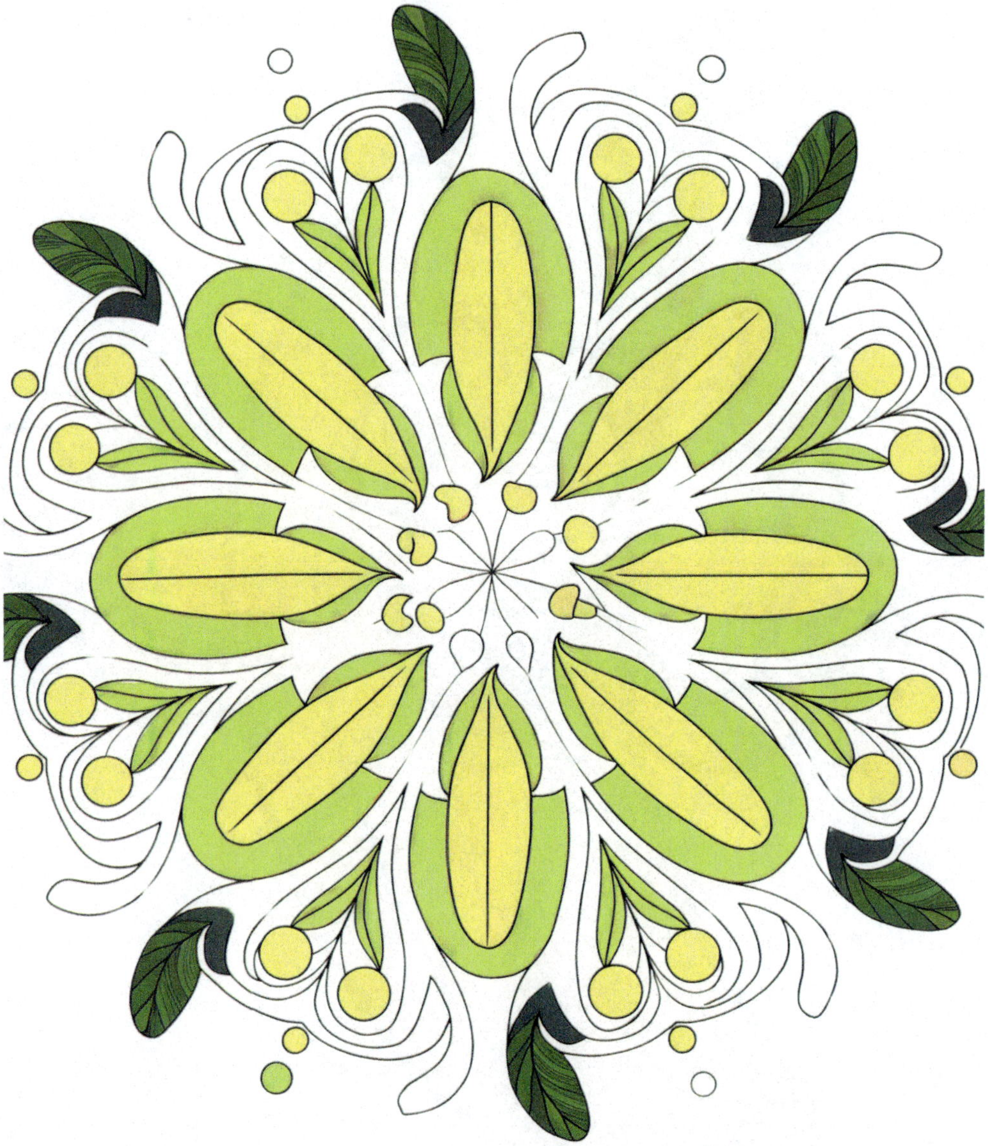

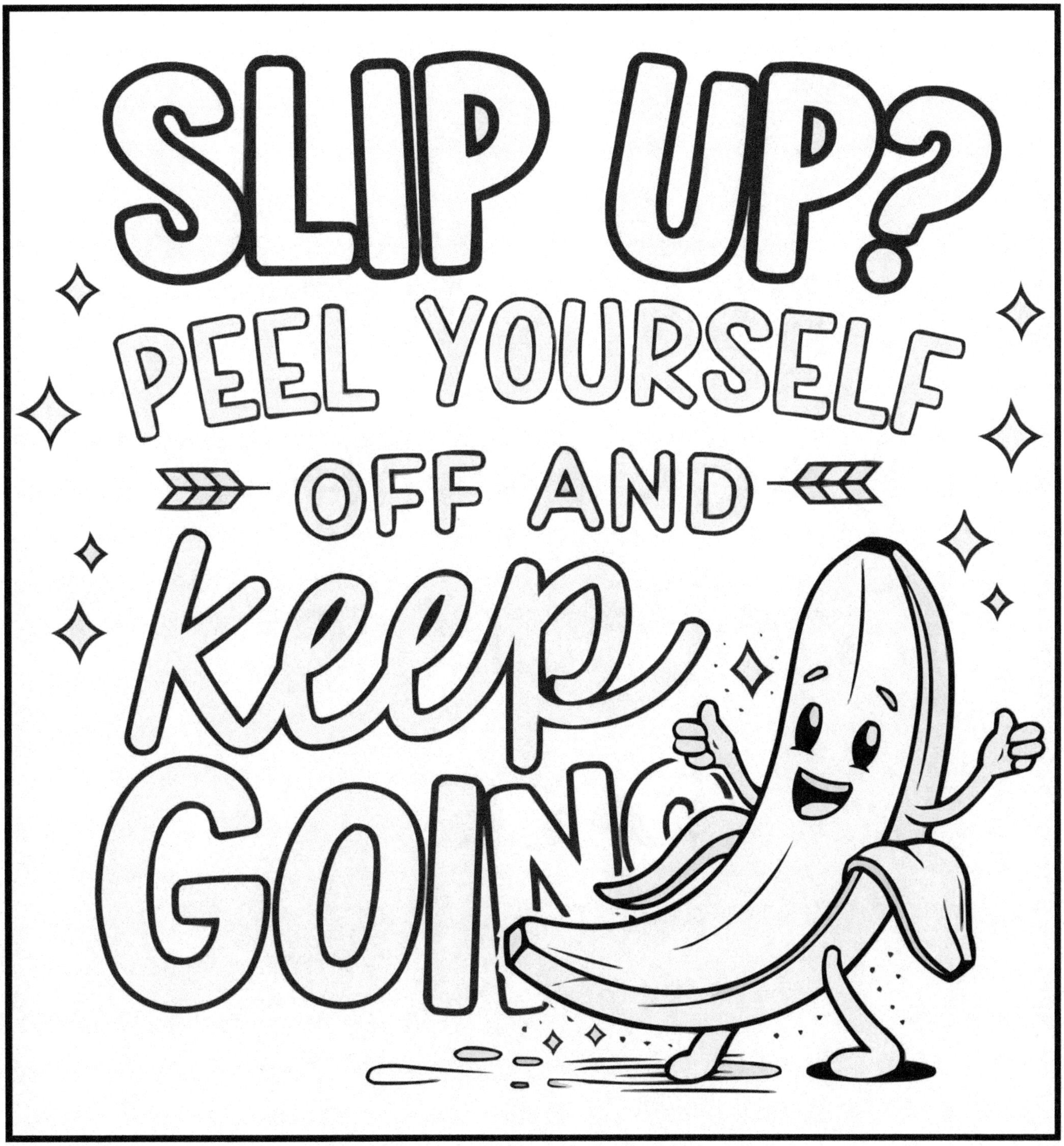
SLIP UP?
PEEL YOURSELF
OFF AND
keep
GOIN

THIS IS THE
BACK OF THE
COLOURING
PAGE

GO BANANAS LIFE'S MORE FUN THAT WAY!

THIS IS THE BACK OF THE COLOURING PAGE

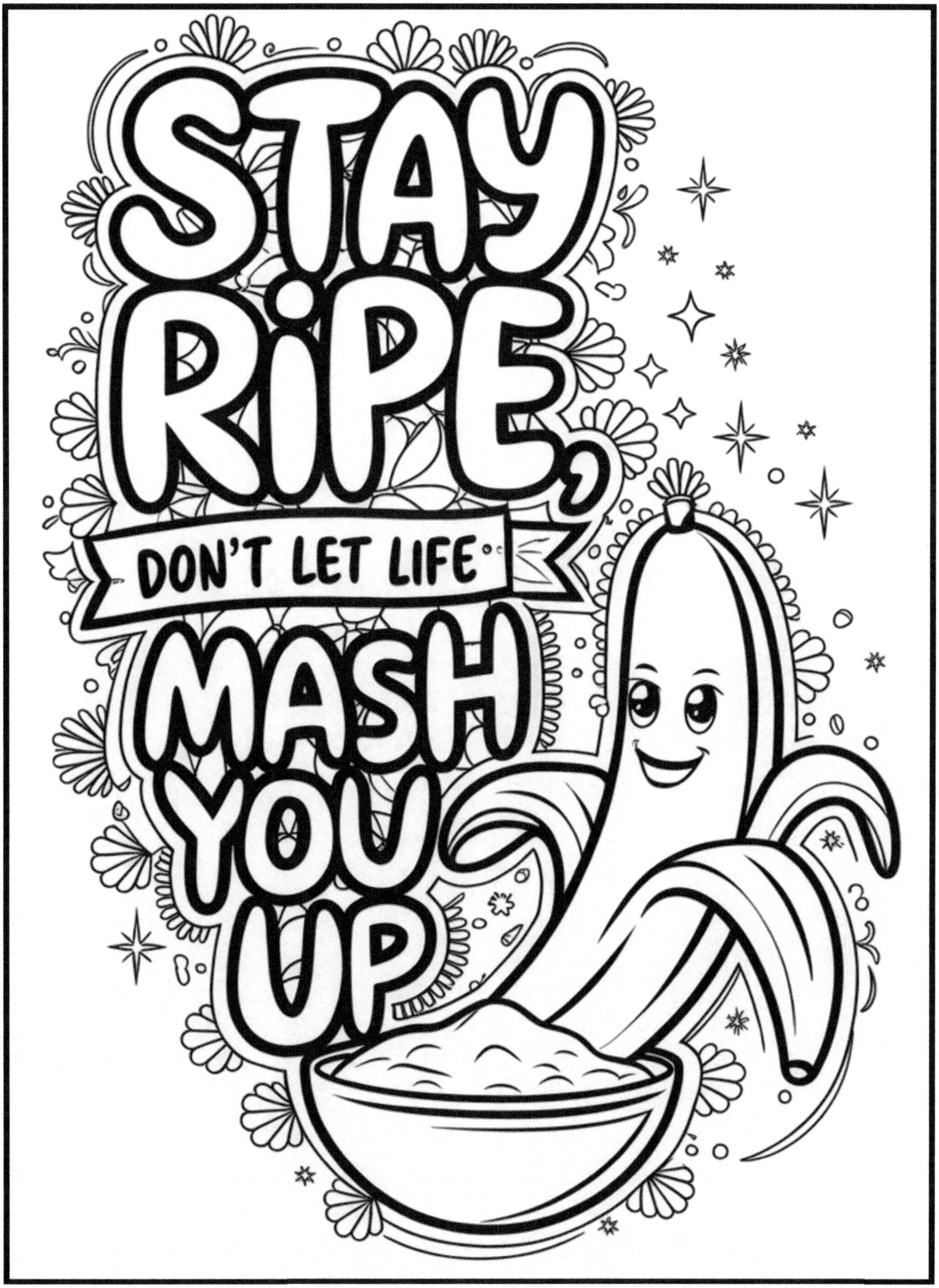
STAY
RIPE,
DON'T LET LIFE
MASH
YOU
UP

THIS IS THE BACK OF THE COLOURING PAGE

If you slip laugh it off and keep climbing

THIS IS THE BACK OF THE COLOURING PAGE

Don't be shy, you've got a lot of a-peel!

THIS IS THE BACK OF THE COLOURING PAGE

Life's a Bunch - B hang in There

THIS IS THE BACK OF THE COLOURING PAGE

YOU'RE THE TOP BANANA, Act like it

THIS IS THE BACK OF THE COLOURING PAGE

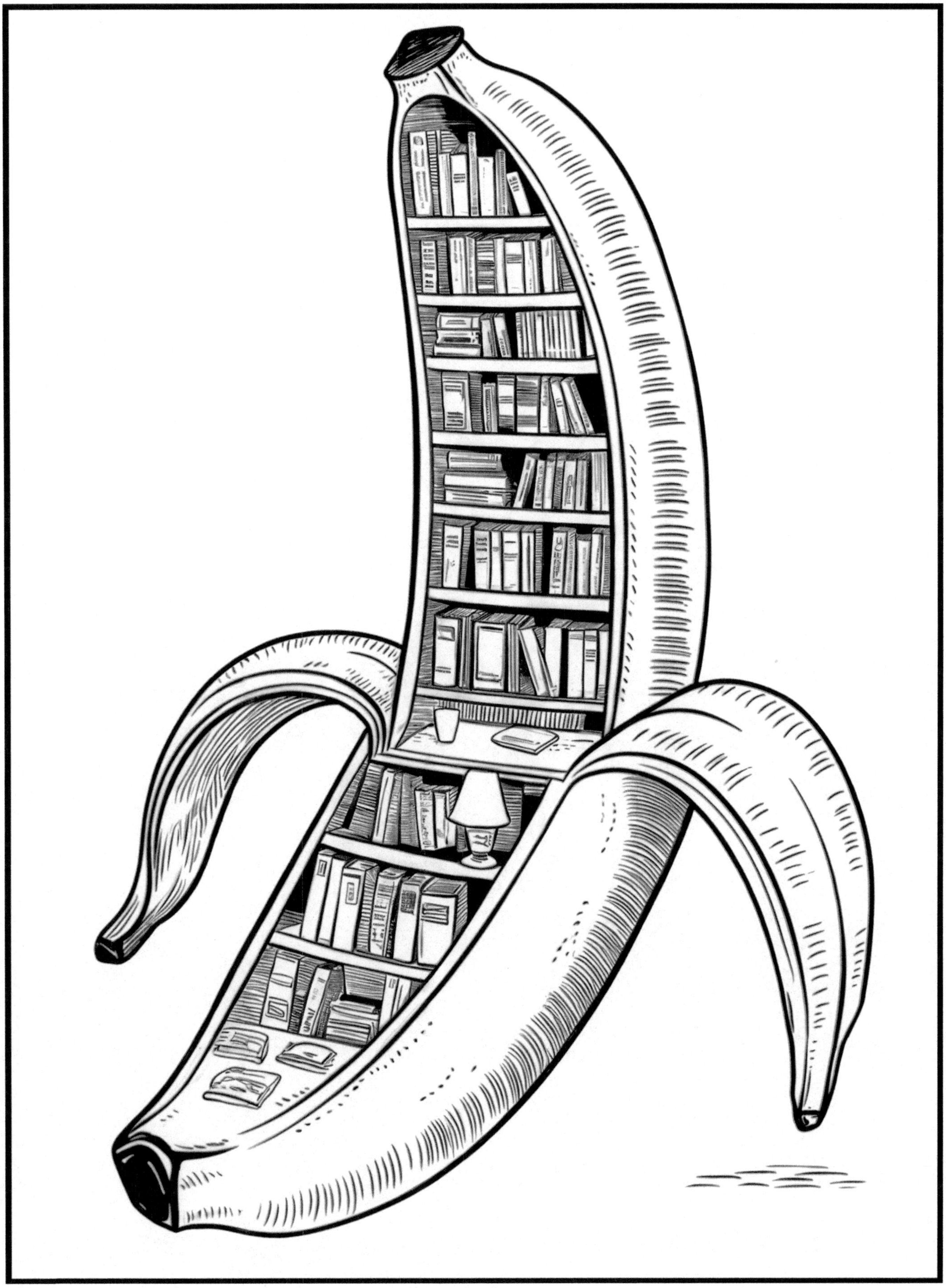

THIS IS THE BACK OF THE COLOURING PAGE

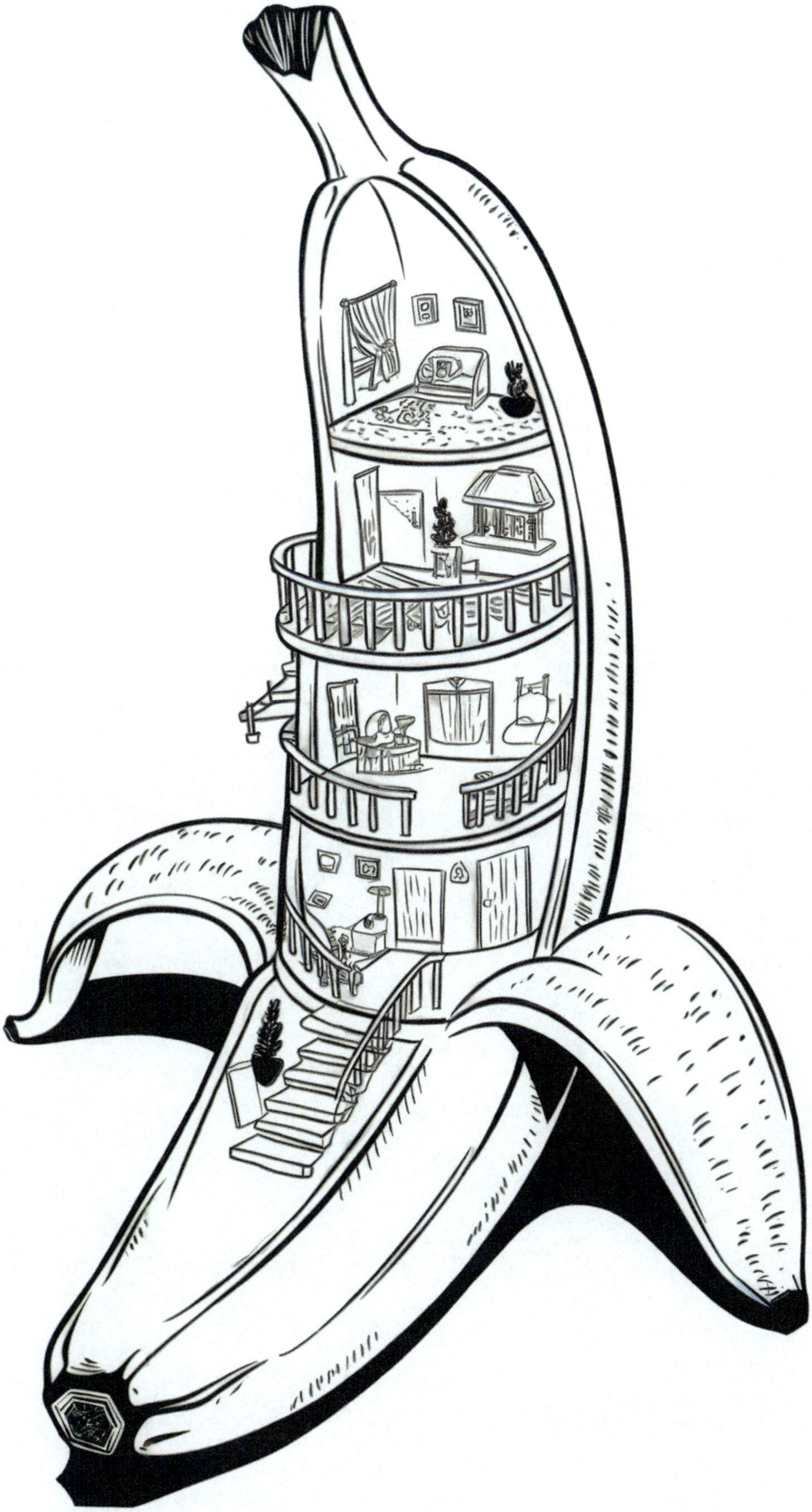

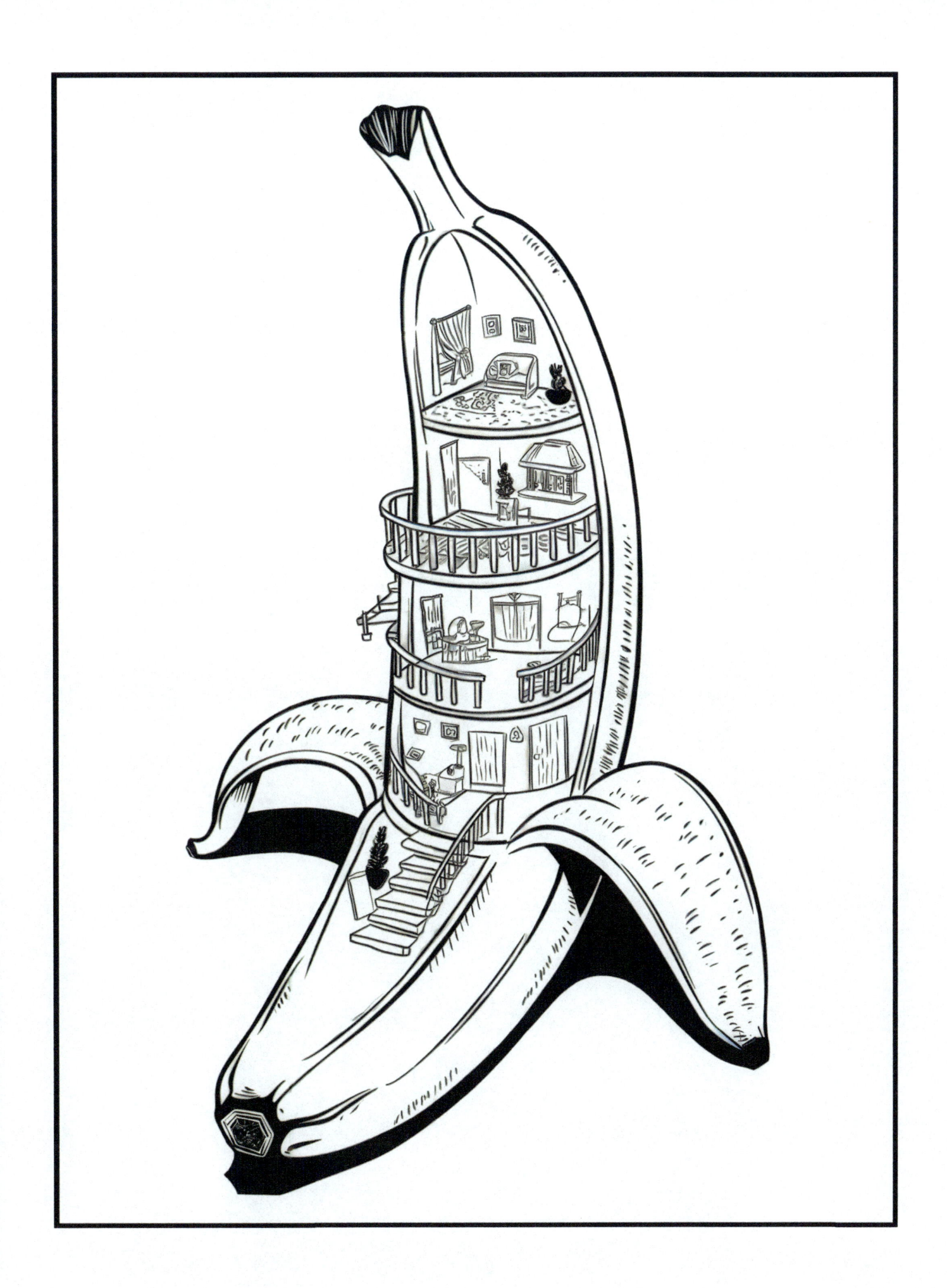

THIS IS THE BACK OF THE COLOURING PAGE

COLOR-BY-BANANA!

Instructions

This might just be the easiest color-by-number you'll ever do! Your mission is simple: grab your yellow crayon or marker and bring this banana to life, one number at a time. Why only one color? Well, because every banana deserves to shine in its true, yellow glory! So go ahead, color it in, and let the fun (and the yellow) begin!

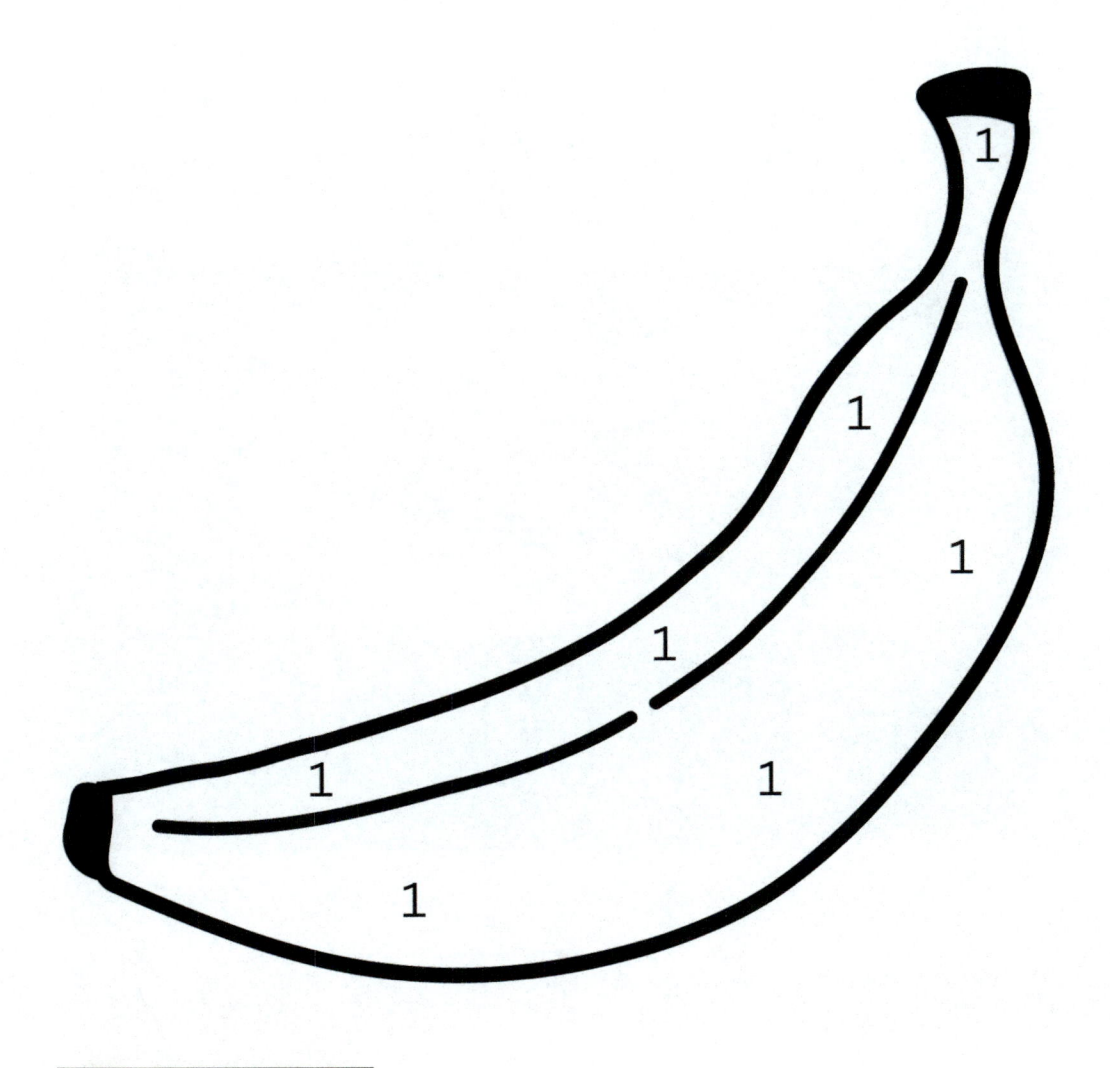

1- yellow

Banana For Mind, Body & Soul

Physical Health Benefits
BANANAS: NATURE'S YELLOW POWERHOUSES!

1 Packed with Potassium

Forget cramping up—bananas are here to save the day with their super potassium powers! Your muscles will thank you.

2 Energy Boosting

Need a quick pick-me-up? Grab a banana! It's like nature's own energy bar, minus the confusing ingredients.

3 Good for the Gut

With all that fiber, bananas help keep your digestion running smoothly. You could say they help you... keep things moving!

4 Heart Healthy

Bananas are heart-friendly, keeping blood pressure in check while tasting way better than any pill.

5 Super Snack for Athletes

It's no wonder athletes love them—bananas give you quick energy and keep you going strong. Plus, they fit perfectly in gym bags!

Mental Health Benefits
BANANAS: A BOOST FOR YOUR BRAIN

Bananas aren't just for fueling your body—they're brain food too! Check out how these yellow wonders keep your mind sharp and stress-free.

1 Mood Lifter

Bananas contain tryptophan, which helps your body produce serotonin, the "feel-good" chemical. So when life gets tough, peel a banana and smile!

2 Stress-Busting Superfruit

Feeling the weight of the world? Bananas are rich in B-vitamins, which help calm your nerves. It's like a little zen in a peel.

3 Memory Power-Up

Need to remember all those important details? The vitamin B6 in bananas helps with brain function, so you'll be the sharpest banana in the bunch!

4 Stay Focused

Bananas help you concentrate and keep your mind clear—perfect for when you need to focus on the important stuff, like finding that last word in a puzzle!

5 Goodbye Anxiety

Bananas help stabilize blood sugar levels, so when life's slipping out of control, they can help you stay balanced

Spiritual Health Benefits
BANANAS: PEEL YOUR WAY TO INNER PEACE!

Yes, even your spirit can benefit from bananas! Here's how this humble fruit helps you find your banana-bliss

1 Banana Meditation
The gentle act of peeling and eating a banana can be a form of mindfulness. Focus on the moment—each bite brings you closer to banana nirvana

2 Grounding Energy
Bananas grow close to the earth, reminding you to stay grounded and connected. When life feels bananas, peel one to center yourself.

3 A Symbol of Resilience
No matter how many times it falls, a banana peel never gives up—it's always ready to slip you up! Take that as a spiritual lesson in resilience.

4 Nurture Your Inner Monkey
Bananas connect us with nature and remind us of our primal roots. Embrace your inner monkey and enjoy the simplicity of life!

5 Peel Away Negativity
As you peel a banana, imagine peeling away all the stress and negativity from your life. You'll feel lighter, both inside and out!

Banana Bites of Knowledge
FUN FACTS TO FUEL YOUR BANANA BRAIN!

"Bananas are actually berries, but strawberries aren't! Nature can be confusing sometimes, huh?"

"There are more than 1,000 different types of bananas! But only a few of them are sold in grocery stores—so much banana variety to explore!"

"Bananas have a natural antacid effect and can help with heartburn. Talk about a superfruit!"

"Bananas are one of the most popular fruits in the world—over 100 billion are eaten every year! That's enough to circle the earth more than 20 times!"

"Bananas grow in bunches called 'hands,' and each individual banana is called a 'finger.' So technically, you've been eating banana fingers all this time!"

Banana Bites of Knowledge
FUN FACTS TO FUEL YOUR BANANA BRAIN!

"Monkeys peel bananas from the bottom up. So if you want to peel like a pro, give it a try!"

"The world record for peeling and eating the most bananas in one minute is 8! Think you can beat that?"

"Bananas float in water because they are less dense than the liquid! They're like the perfect little yellow boats."

"In Japan, there's a type of banana called the 'Musa Banana' whose peel is so thin, people eat it whole—peel and all!"

"The largest banana bunch ever grown contained 473 bananas and weighed over 130 pounds! That's a serious banana bonanza!"

Banana Yoga

Important *Note*

The yoga poses in this book, including the Scorpion Banana Pose (Banana Tail Flip), are intended for entertainment and fun! They are not meant to be used as professional exercise guidance.

1. Safety First: Always consult a qualified instructor before attempting any yoga poses, especially those that involve bending or stretching like the Scorpion Banana Pose (Banana Tail Flip).
2. For Laughs, Not Labs: These poses are part of the book's banana-themed fun and are best enjoyed as illustrations—not instructions.

Remember, even bananas know when to take a break. Enjoy the humor and inspiration, but leave the actual stretching to the pros! 🍌🧘‍♀️

Cobra Banana

PEEL UP POSE

Banana Dish Pose

THE BANANA BOAT

Downward Dog Banana

BANANA SPLIT STRETCH

Scorpion Banana

BANANA TAIL FLIP

Solutions

Banana Facts or Fiction?
ANSWERS

1. Some people believe that the potassium in banana peels helps whiten teeth. While there's no solid scientific proof, it's a popular home remedy!

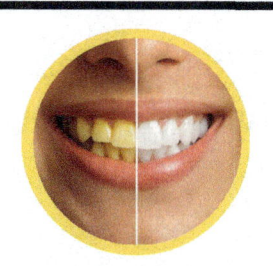

   FACT

2. While there are some varieties of bananas that are red or purple, the common yellow banana starts green and ripens to yellow.

   FICTION

3. The banana plant is classified as an herbaceous plant because its stem does not contain true woody tissue.

   FACT

4. Bananas don't sing, but that would make for some interesting fruit conversations!

   FICTION

5. Bananas contain tryptophan and magnesium, which are natural muscle relaxants and can make you feel drowsy.

   FACT

Banana Facts or Fiction?
ANSWERS

6. Bananas are tropical plants and definitely don't grow in freezing Antarctica!

FICTION

7. The word "banana" actually comes from the Arabic word "banan," meaning finger, because bananas are shaped like fingers.

FICTION

8. Bananas are rich in vitamin B6, which helps the body produce serotonin and regulate mood.

FACT

9. Bananas don't grow that fast! While they grow quickly, they don't reach 3 inches per day.

FICTION

10. In parts of ancient Africa, bananas were used as a form of barter and trade due to their value as a food source.

FACT

You Nailed It—Banana Style!

Congratulations, you've gone totally bananas! As you might have guessed (or maybe not?), every answer was the one and only—banana! Whether you knew it from the start or had to peel back a few hints, we hope you had a bunch of fun. Remember, when in doubt, the answer is always… you guessed it—banana!

1 What fruit is known for making people slip in cartoons?

a) Banana
b) Banana
c) Banana

2 Which fruit is often used in smoothies and breakfast bowls?

a) Banana
b) Banana
c) Banana

3 Which fruit can be found in bunches and is packed with potassium?

a) Banana
b) Banana
c) Banana

4 What fruit would you most likely see in a tropical jungle?

a) Banana
b) Banana
c) Banana

5 What fruit is the main ingredient in a banana split?

a) Banana
b) Banana
c) Banana

6 Which fruit is famous for being both a healthy snack and a comedy prop?

a) Banana
b) Banana
c) Banana

7 Which fruit do athletes love for a quick energy boost?

a) Banana
b) Banana
c) Banana

8 What fruit do monkeys love to munch on?

a) Banana
b) Banana
c) Banana

BANANA DAY

Go Bananas!

CROSSWORD # 3 Answers

Answer #1

1 B
2 B
3 B
4 BANANA
5 BANANA
6 BANANA

Answer #2

1 B
2 B
3 B
4 BANANA
5 BANANA
6 BANANA

Answer #3

1 B
2 B
3 BANANA
4 B
5 BANANA
6 BANANA

Answer #4

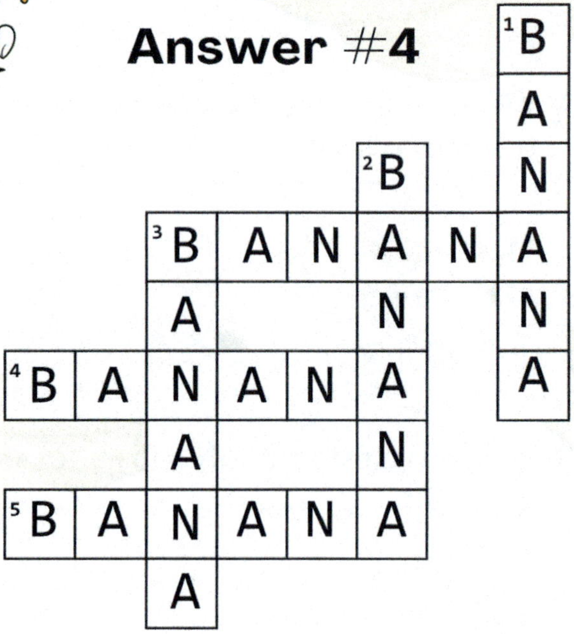
1 B
2 B
3 BANANA
4 BANANA
5 BANANA

Banana Revealed: The Big Peel
ANSWERS

Answer#1

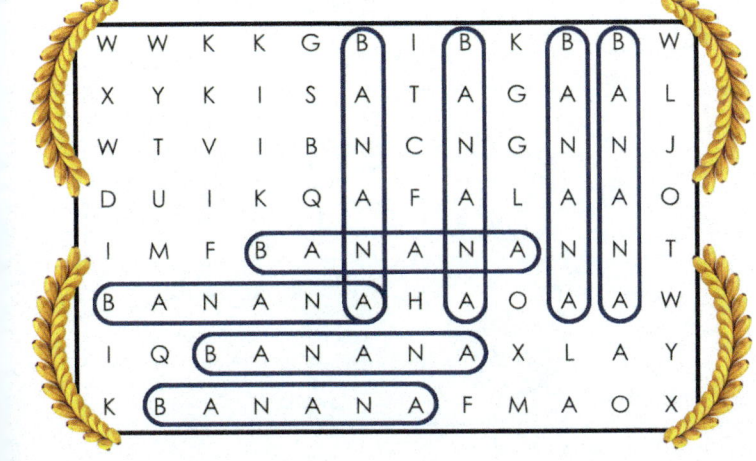

Answer#2

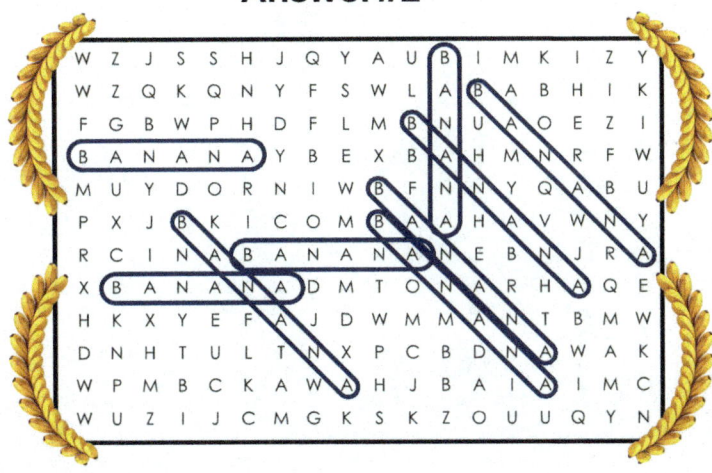

Answer#3

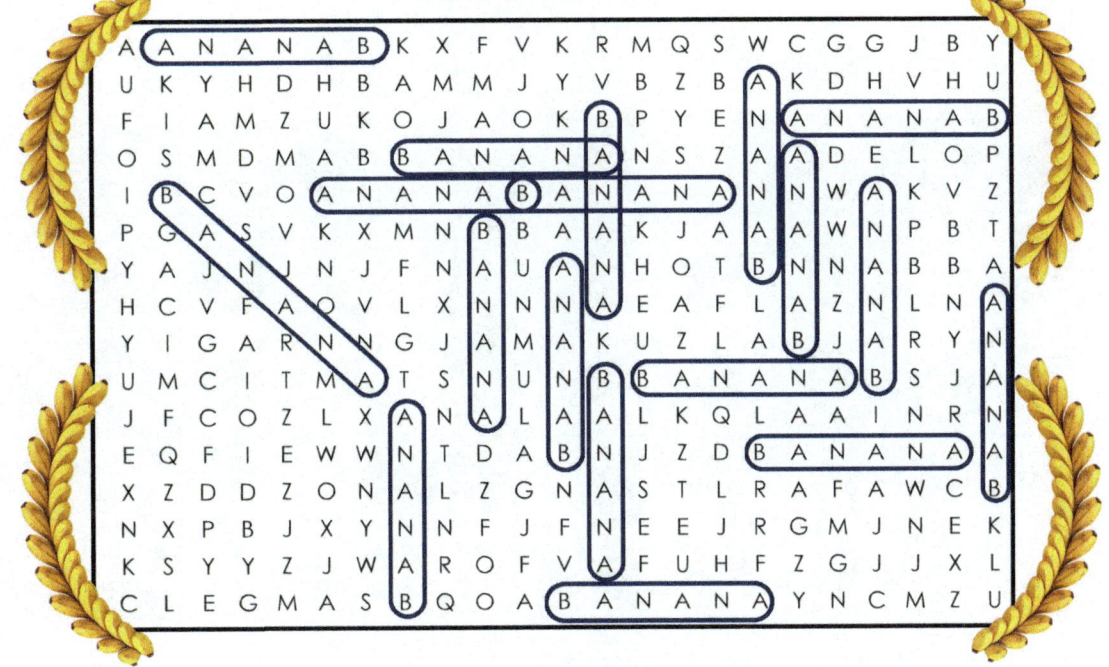

69

SUDOKU Answers

4X4

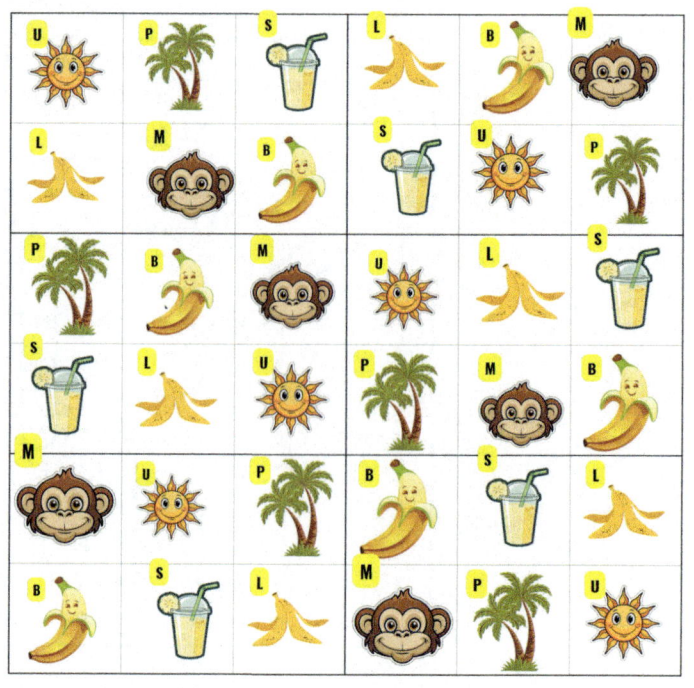

Answer #1

M	S	B	P
P	B	M	S
B	P	S	M
S	M	P	B

Answer #2

P	B	M	S
M	S	B	P
B	P	S	M
S	M	P	B

6X6

Answer #1

L	B	U	M	P	S
S	M	P	B	L	U
U	P	L	S	M	B
B	S	M	P	U	L
P	U	S	L	B	M
M	L	B	U	S	P

Answer #2

U	P	S	L	B	M
L	M	B	U	S	P
P	B	M	U	L	S
S	L	U	P	M	B
M	S	P	B	U	L
B	U	L	M	P	U

70

SUDOKU Answers

9X9

Answer #1

Answer #2

71

Get Certified

Certificate of Completion

Congratulations, Your name here

banana-bonkers

Course completed on November 26, 2024

Instructor
Moodgee Banana

Visit Moodgee.com/banana-bonkers/ or scan the QR code below to download your exclusive Certificate of Completion

scan me >>

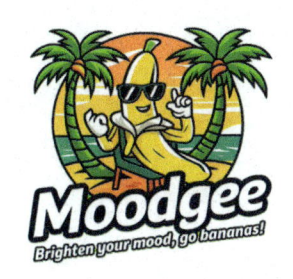

Thank you

We hope you had a blast solving puzzles, laughing at jokes, and unleashing your creativity with our banana-themed adventures! Your journey doesn't end here—Moodgee has so much more in store! We'd love to hear your thoughts and see how much fun you had. Please consider leaving a review to let others know how this book made you smile, think, and go bananas!

Ready for more banana-tastic surprises? More activities that we couldn't fit in the book. Visit **Moodgee.com** or scan the QR code below to download more printable activities, listen to the catchy Moodgee song, and explore more about living a balanced, joy-filled life. We're always working on new and exciting books, so stay tuned and keep peeling back the layers of fun with Moodgee!

scan me >>

Banana Sudoku Stickers

ICONS SYMBOLS

4X4 PUZZLE #1

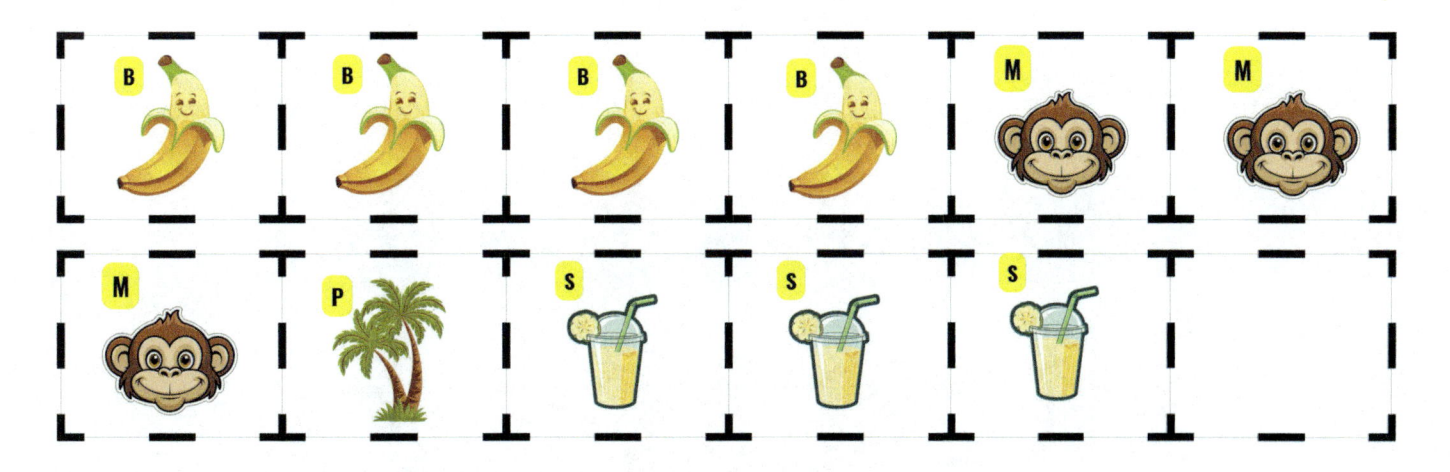

B B B B M M
M P S S S

4X4 PUZZLE #2

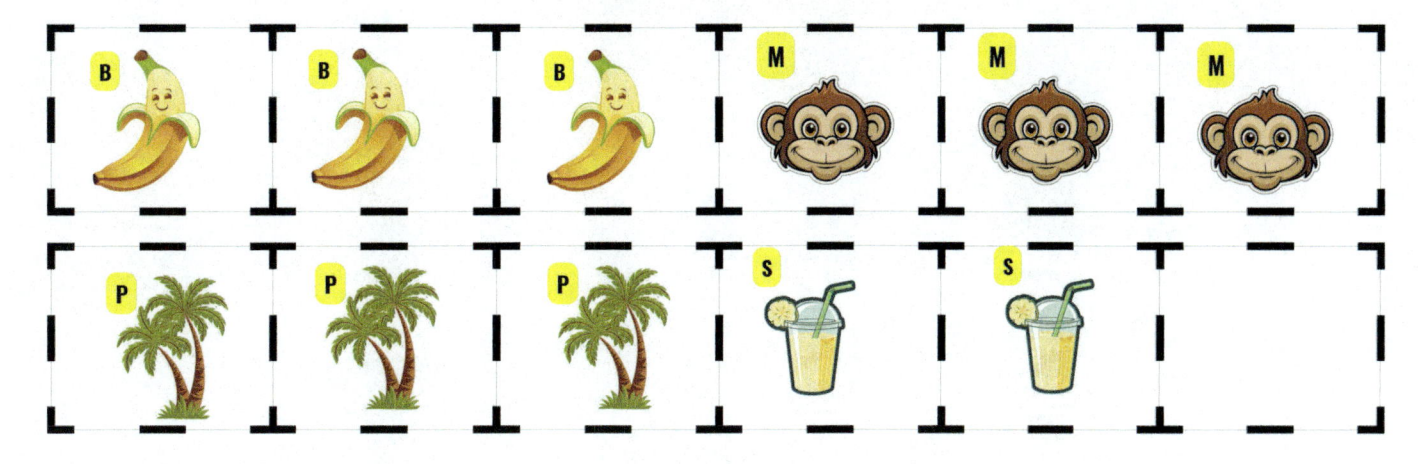

B B B M M M
P P P S S

THIS IS THE

BACK OF THE

STICKERS PAGE

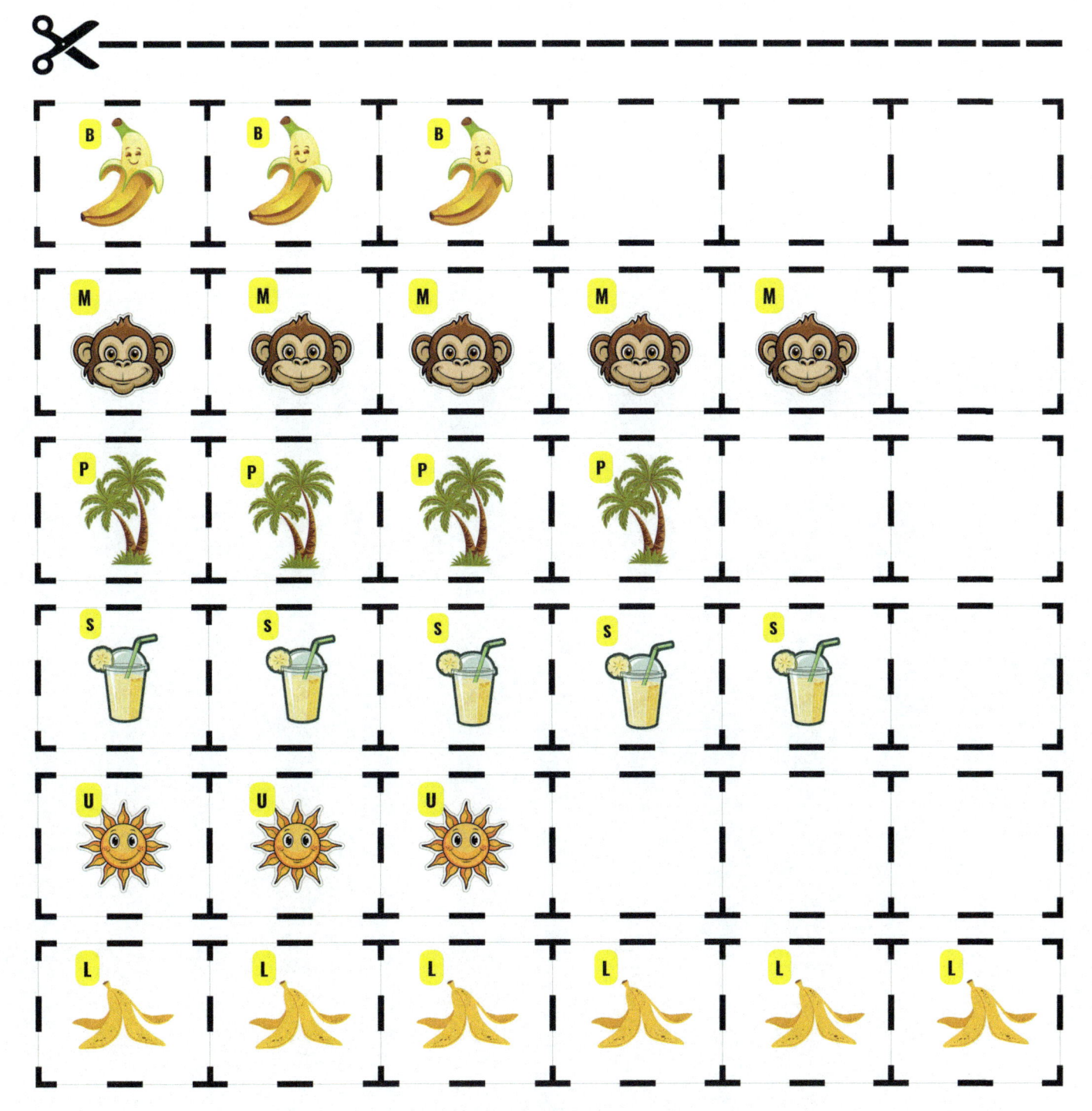

ICONS SYMBOLS

77

THIS IS THE

BACK OF THE

STICKERS PAGE

ICONS SYMBOLS

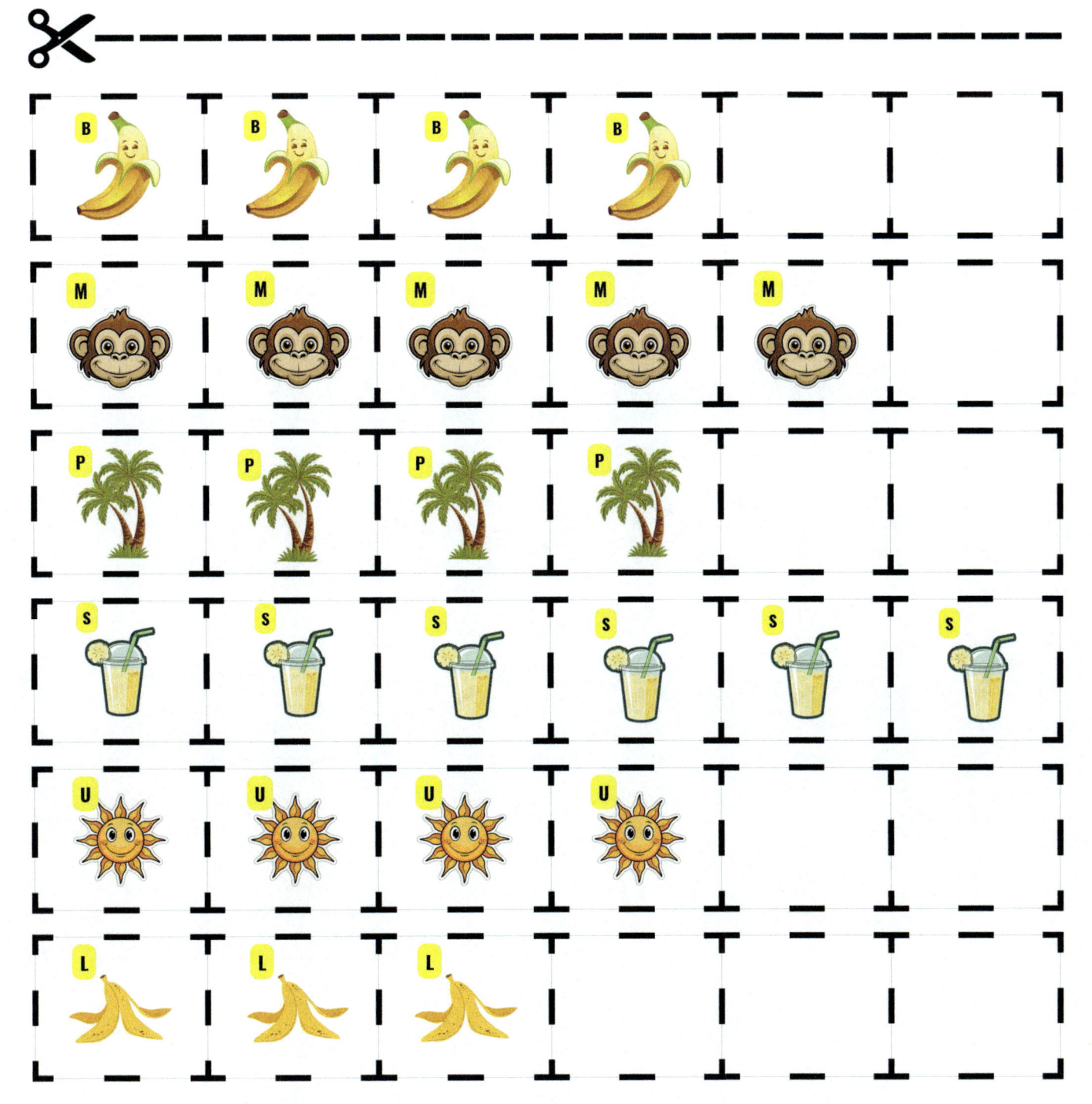

B	B	B	B		
M	M	M	M	M	
P	P	P	P		
S	S	S	S	S	S
U	U	U	U		
L	L	L			

THIS IS THE

BACK OF THE

STICKERS PAGE

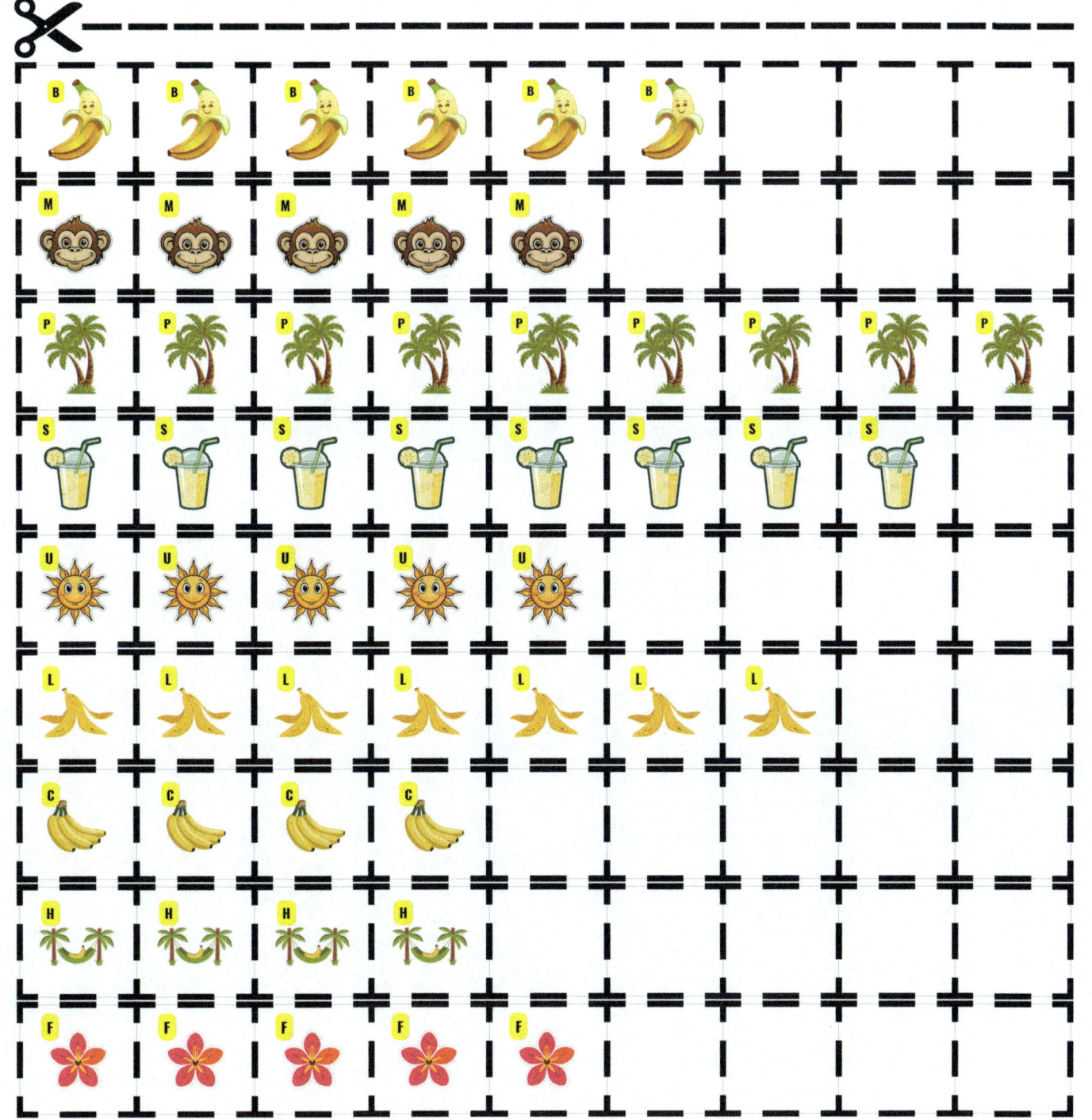

ICONS SYMBOLS

THIS IS THE

BACK OF THE

STICKERS PAGE

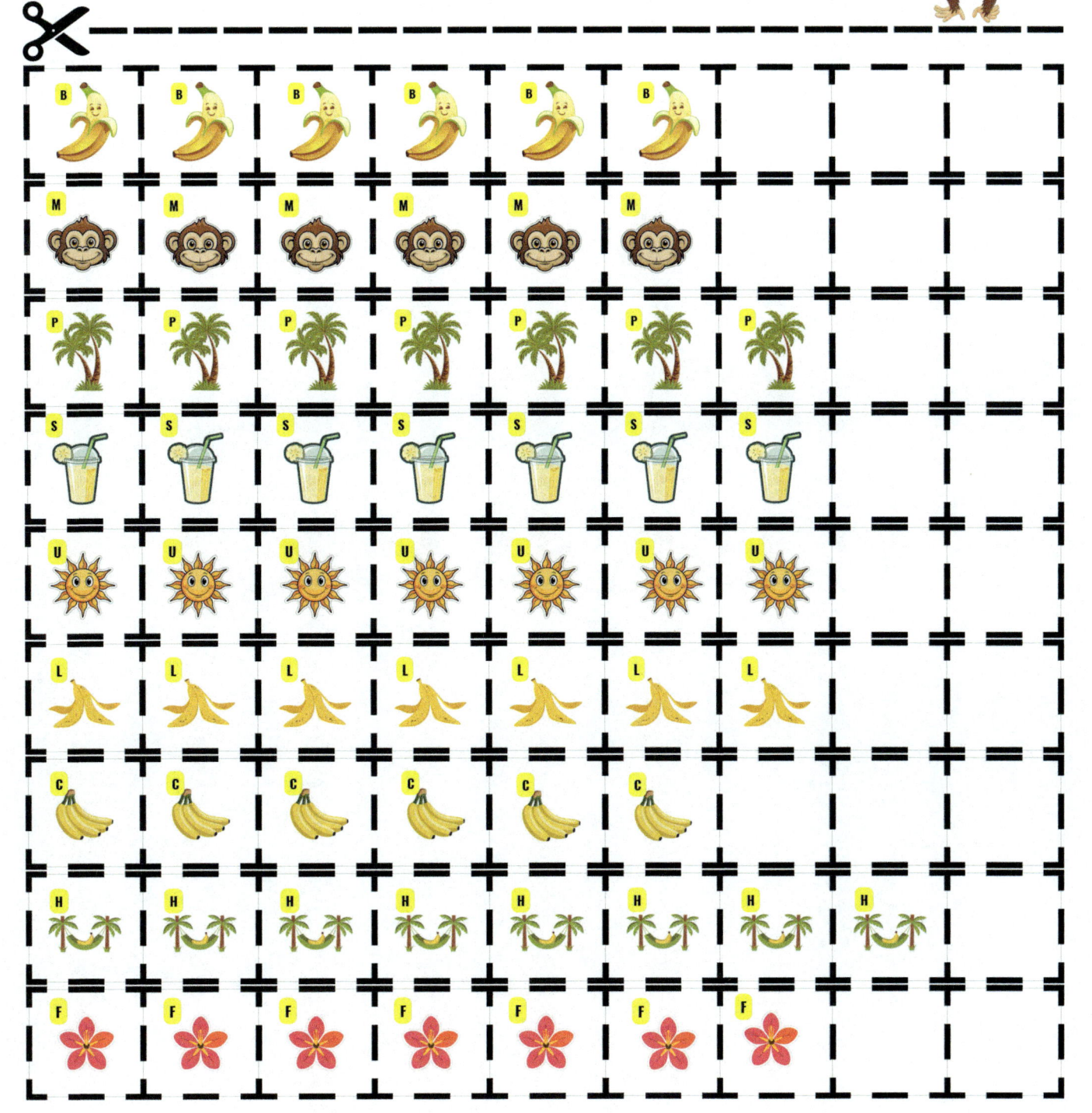

ICONS SYMBOLS

THIS IS THE

BACK OF THE

STICKERS PAGE

Printed in Great Britain
by Amazon

56501305R00051